True Worthy Hoit

The Right of American Slavery

True Worthy Hoit

The Right of American Slavery

ISBN/EAN: 9783743321403

Manufactured in Europe, USA, Canada, Australia, Japa

Cover: Foto ©ninafisch / pixelio.de

Manufactured and distributed by brebook publishing software
(www.brebook.com)

True Worthy Hoit

The Right of American Slavery

RIGHT

OF

AMERICAN SLAVERY.

BY

T. W. HOYT,

OF THE ST. LOUIS LITERARY AND PHILOSOPHICAL ASSOCIATION.

SOUTHERN AND WESTERN EDITION.

FIRST AND SECOND EDITIONS, 500,000 COPIES.

FOR SALE BY THE PRINCIPAL PUBLISHERS THROUGHOUT THE UNION

ST. LOUIS, MO.:
PUBLISHED BY L. BUSHNELL.
1860.

PREFACE.

To the American People.

My Fellow Countrymen : — Upon what manner of times have we fallen? Is our supposed experiment of self-government about to prove a failure? Are we so blind as not to see the abyss into which we are about to plunge? Section hostile against section; States arrayed against the Constitution; Churches sundered; the springs of intelligence poisoned at their source; treason stalking at noonday; insurrection rife; the equality of States and citizens denied, and derided; justice rebuked; treachery applauded; traitors canonized; anarchy inaugurated; monarchy calculating the end of republicanism; and the wheels of government clogged by the minions of despotism! All this, my Countrymen, and you passive, silent, sightless; reckless of your own and your children's doom? And while all this is true, you go about your usual avocations, as though the eyes of the civilized world were not upon you; as though the great, the good, the magnanimous of all lands were not breathless, and spell-bound, and appalled at the spectacle; as though the prophetic admonitions of the Father of our Country were forgotten, and nature, with an ominous silence, conspired to lull you into forgetfulness, the more to astound you with the wonders and the woes of an approaching catastrophe!

What fatal error is there in our Republican principle? What virus sickens our body politic? What fascination lures us from the shrine of freedom? What infatuation hath seized the American people, that they should put to hazard this priceless inheritance,—the home, and refuge, and hope, of the down-trodden nations?

I aver there is a fatal fallacy adopted by a large number of the American people, which, if not rejected, will lead us down to national oblivion. That fallacy is exposed in the following pages, by showing what is right, and what is wrong, and explaining the fundamental error by which our public opinion is divided, and the way of a reunion pointed out. No one can desire to remain in error. It is the desire to do right which animates the great mass of the American people. It was, perhaps, the *desire* to do right, that made John Brown a rebel and a traitor, and which consigned

5

him to a traitor's doom. There is no safety, then, in *desiring* to do right; but to KNOW what is right, and to DO it. The time has now arrived when the American people must do right, or suffer the penalty of doing wrong.

Good *intentions* will not do. Good DEEDS are demanded,—actions founded upon truth and justice, and in accordance with nature's irrevocable laws. We boast of our greatness, and power, and intelligence. Of what avail are all these, if they will not save us from national ruin? What boots it that a slumbering giant dreams of his strength while he is falling upon the bosom of a burning lake? The mightiest empires have sunk to oblivion. Are we soon to follow them?

Our material greatness and vigor seem to forbid the idea of premature decay; but let us not be blind to the delusive dream of an immortality springing from mental imbecility, nor the chimera of a political finality in governmental system which establishes and tolerates INJUSTICE, nor the permanence of a State in the midst of preponderating elements of fluctuating popular delusion.

Either the institutions under which we live are founded in truth, or they are founded in error. Our constitution is the work of wisdom, or of folly. It is founded in justice, or injustice; in RIGHT, or *wrong.*

Shall we honor the astuteness of its founders, and perpetuate these institutions to remotest ages? or shall we prove recreant to this trust, unworthy of these manifold blessings, and in our mental blindness and moral imbecility invoke the scorn of future ages, and the just execrations of all mankind?

The *material* elements of greatness of the Great American Republic, must be vivified and enlivened by a corresponding degree of INTELLECT; they must be permeated by an adequate element of illuminating soul, or they will fall, a lifeless mass, into chaotic ruin. Let us remember

> "That trade's proud empire hastes to swift decay,
> As ocean sweeps the labored mole away;
> Whilst self-dependent power can time defy,
> As rocks resist the billows and the sky."

THE RIGHT OF SLAVERY.

INTRODUCTION.

AFRICAN SLAVERY is, at present, the subject of all-absorbing interest to the American mind; for, our people, almost intoxicated with their own freedom, seem unsatisfied with those manifold blessings acquired by the labors of their sires; and while they are conscious of not excelling them in wisdom, virtue, or valor, they are becoming ideal, and seem willing to sacrifice the practical, safe rules of republican action, for mere idealisms, born in the dizzy sphere of their own over-wrought imaginations. They tremble at the name of Washington, whose purity and moral power shed lustre upon the name of man, and they worship him as a god; but while the REAL WASHINGTON commands the homage of mankind, and stands the intermediate between the race of men and the Infinite, we find the imaginations of men ignoring reason, and embarked upon a voyage aerial, amid the clouds. There they revel high above the mountain tops of Washington, Jefferson, and Franklin, where the atmosphere is pure, where the light is clear, and where the lightnings play; but, alas for human weakness and frailty! they are there only in imagination, though the splendid illusion is to them a reality, and the pleasing dream of ideal beauty, which, by the magic power of transmutation, annihilates or obliterates the reason and memory, destroys those distinctions of great and little, right and wrong, weakness and power, which nature has arbitrarily made, and the experience of mankind recognized as fundamental; upon which all law is based, and all order and civilization sustained and advanced, for the security and elevation of nations and of men.

8

THE IDEAL AND THE REAL.

This ideal element so predominates, in consequence of over or false *culture;* by the reading of a spurious literature, which dwells in the regions of fiction and romance, to the proportionate neglect of the stirring incidents of our time, which actually go to make up true history—which seem marvellous enough of themselves, without the necessity of invention, or the aid of artificial novelties, except for mere embellishment.

It would seem that the rise and progress of this Republic; the spread of our ocean commerce; the building of a thousand cities; the rush of the world to our shores; the peopling of our boundless plains; the rapid birth of new States into our Union; the triumph of our arms; our repeated accessions of territory; our maritime and commercial superiority; our foreign discoveries; our inventions in mechanism; our discoveries in science; the use of steam, and electricity; our statesmanship, and foreign diplomacy; a thousand miraculous incidents of individual enterprise and success; the discovery of gold, of silver, and iron; our internal improvements and meliorations; our national *prestige;* and finally, our greatness and glory as a nation,—ought to suffice for any reasonable conception of the marvellous, as they outstrip the more ignoble creations of fancy, and absolutely invade the former domain of fiction and romance. Hence the seeming puerility of fiction when contrasted with these more wondrous phenomena of fact. The substitution of fiction for fact is, therefore, unnecessary and absurd, as it defeats the very purpose intended, by its own inferiority. Its chief effect, then, is but to mislead the mind.

Let us, then, control the imagination; discard the *ideal* in practical affairs, hold it in its sphere, and adopt the REAL, in order that by the exercise of right reason we may be enabled to consider the present subject as it *is,* and not as it would be when weighed in the scale of the ideal; for in this way, and this alone, can we come to just conclusions, and our labors result in practical benefit to those most concerned in the premises. In the spirit of truth, of candor, of sober reality, let us, therefore, approach the subject of American Slavery.

THE NEGRO EVER A SLAVE.

The Negro has been a slave from time immemorial. This is shown from the earliest Egyptian monuments, paintings, and traditions. Herodotus, the father of Grecian History, tells us of negro slavery in Ancient Greece. It existed in Rome also. During the tenth century of the Christian era, the Moors, from Barbary, established an extensive traffic in the cities of Nigritia, where they bought large numbers of slaves; and the merchants of Seville brought slaves from the western coast of Africa, and established slavery in that city, and in Andalusia, long before the time of Columbus.* It is also a curious fact in history, that Hanno, the great Carthagenian commander and discoverer, having explored Africa from the Straits of Gibraltar to the bounds of Arabia, brought back to Carthage a cargo of ourang-outangs, which he supposed to be Negro men and women ; *showing more historically his estimate of African character, than his familiarity with Natural History.* The Negro has ever been a slave;† and it is to be considered whether his quick and sudden transition from slavery to freedom, by emancipation, is probable or possible, or is sanctioned by the history of human development and progress.

* Leo Africanus says, Book vii., "The King of Borno sent for the merchants of Barbary, and willed them to bring him great store of horses ; for in this country they used to exchange horses for slaves, and to give fifteen and sometimes twenty slaves for one horse ; and by this means there were abundance of horses brought ; howbeit, the merchants were constrained to stay for their slaves till the king returned home with a great number of captives, and satisfied his creditors for their horses." "The king maketh invasions but every year once, and that at one set and appointed time of the year."—*Geogr. Hist. of Africa, trans. by Pory, pp.* 293, 294, *Lon.*, 1600.

† "From Abyssinia, the caravans carry yearly to Cairo nearly two thousand Negroes, those poor creatures having unfortunately been captured in war. Most of the chiefs and sovereigns in the interior of Africa sell or put to death all their prisoners."—*Narrative of a Ten Years' Residence at Tripoli, p.* 185, *London*, 1816.

TWO PHASES OF SLAVERY.

Slavery has two phases; the moral, which involves the RIGHT, and the prudential, which is the expedient. But strictly, the moral is the principal and controlling view of the subject, and that which has made and will continually constitute the criterion of action from which the expediency is deduced, and the anomaly of slavery in our Republic understood, the paradox of a slave-holding democracy explained, and the institution of slavery justified with human equality, by justly discriminating between barbarism and humanity, civilization and savagism, justice and injustice, right and wrong.

THE RIGHT OF SLAVERY.

I assert the right and justice of slavery, and found my arguments on the subject in right alone. If it can be shown to be right, then it is expedient; if wrong, then it cannot be shown to be expedient, and, if possible, it ought to be abolished. It is the *idea* of the *wrong* of slavery which has misled, and is continuing to mislead, the American mind.

By what process of reasoning, then, can slavery be shown to be just? I answer, because RIGHT holds a just and hereditary control over *wrong*. I answer, that it is right that barbarism should subserve civilization. I assert that barbarism is *wrong*, and civilization is RIGHT; that the former conduces to the misery and the latter to the happiness of mankind. Barbarism—with its pagan idolatries, its monstrous superstitions, its devil-worship, its false religious rites, its heathen orgies, its cruelties, its canni-balism—is wrong. Who will deny this? Who are its apologists and advocates? Let them stand forth and show the right of barbarism! Let us have a homily on its beauties! let them pic-ture to us the meliorations of cannibalism! Will any one do it? No; it is a self-evident wrong. To attempt, even, to prove it wrong, would seem to be a work of supererogation. Barbarism is repugnant to the common sense of the Anglo-Saxon race; a violation of the conscience of civilization. Cannibalism is an almost inconceivable outrage against all right, in moral, social, or even superior animal existence. Few animals or even reptiles devour their kind. It is, therefore, an act repugnant to human nature, and in violation of the amenities even of a nobler animal existence. In a word, it is unmitigated wrong, showing its subjects and votaries to be incarnate devils.

BARBARISM OF THE AFRICAN RACE.

The African race is a race of barbarians, and civilization to that race would be an artificial state of existence.* The vestiges of barbarism characterize the African, in his normal state. The latent principle of cannibalism, lurks, in dormant energy, within the very core of his being, and constitutes a prominent character-

* Hegel, the distinguished German philosopher, in his Philosophy of History, says, pp. 102, 103:

An English traveler states that when a war is determined on in Ashantee, solemn ceremonies precede it. Among other things, the bones of the king's mother are laved with human blood. As a prelude to the war, the king ordains an onslaught upon his own metropolis, as if to excite the due degree of frenzy.

In Dahomey, when the king dies, the bonds of society are loosed; in his palace begins indiscriminate havoc and disorganization. All the wives of the king (in Dahomey their number is exactly 3,333) are massacred, and through the whole town plunder and carnage run riot. The wives of the king regard their death as a necessity; they go richly attired to meet it. The authorities have to hasten to proclaim the new governor, simply to put a stop to massacre.

The only essential connection that has existed and continued between the Negroes and Europeans is that of slavery. In this the Negroes see nothing unbecoming them; and the English, who have done most for abolishing the slave trade and slavery, are treated by the Negroes themselves as enemies. For it is a point of first importance with the kings to sell their captured enemies, or even their own subjects; and viewed in the light of such facts, we may conclude *slavery* to have been the occasion of the increase of human feeling among the Negroes.

Tyranny is regarded as no wrong, and *cannibalism is looked upon as quite customary and proper.* Among us, instinct deters from it, if we can speak of instinct at all as appertaining to man. But with the Negro this is not the case, and the *devouring of human flesh is altogether consonant with the general principles of the African race;* to the sensual Negro, human flesh is but an object of sense,—mere flesh. At the death of a king, hundreds are killed and eaten; prisoners are butchered, *and their flesh is sold in the markets.* The victor is accustomed to eat the heart of his slain foe. When magical rites are performed, it frequently happens that the sorcerer kills the first that comes in his way, *and divides his body among the bystanders.*

istic of his animal existence. The economy and order of nature is
no less marked in the *carnivorous* than in the herbivorous mam-
malia and quadrumana; and although their physical distinctions
are not always so marked as to render apparent, to superficial
observation, the uses and functions of their entire organism, yet
science has been a tolerably faithful interpreter of cause and
effect, and has not failed to recognize those organic qualities, and
the structural adaptability of the African race, which qualify it
for its mission as the representative of barbaric fury and degradation, and the type, in human form, of that chaotic element of
self-annihilation, which nature has kindly restricted to the fewest
number of the lowest orders of animated being.* The inhabitants of Southern and Central Africa, from whence our slaves
are drawn, the Feejeean, the Caffrarian, the New-Zealander, and
the Hottentot, are stamped by nature with the unmistakable
character of unmitigated barbarism, and absolute antagonism to
civilization; and their improvement when brought in contact

* Says Herder,—But the peculiar formation of the members of the human
body says more than all these; and this appears to me applicable in the African
organization. According to various physiological observations, the lips, breasts, and
private parts, are proportionate to each other; and as nature, agreeably to the sim-
ple principle of her plastic art, must have conferred on these people, to whom she
was obliged to deny nobler gifts, an ampler measure of sensual enjoyment, this could
not but have appeared to the physiologist. *According to the rules of physiognomy,
thick lips are held to indicate a sensual disposition;* as thin lips, displaying a slender,
rosy line, are deemed symptoms of chaste and delicate taste; not to mention other
circumstances. *What wonder, then, that in a nation for whom the sensual appetite is
the height of happiness, external marks of it should appear?* A Negro child is born
white; the skin round the nails, the nipples, and private parts, first become colored;
and the same consent of parts in the disposition to color is observable in other
nations. *A hundred children are a trifle to a Negro; and an old man who had not
above seventy, lamented his fate with tears.*
With this oleaginous organization to sensual pleasure, the profile and whole
frame of the body must alter. *The projection of the mouth would render the nose
short and small, the forehead would incline backwards, and the face would have at
a distance the resemblance of that of an ape.* Conformably to this would be the
position of the neck, the transition to the occiput, and the elastic structure of the
whole body, which is formed, even to the nose and skin, for sensual, animal enjoyment.—*Herder's Philosophy of the History of Man, pp.* 150, 151. *Translated by
Churchill, London,* 1800.

with civilization is so slow as almost to escape detection. Indeed it is doubtful whether the arts of European and American civilization have succeeded in so fascinating the African race among us as to warrant the expectation of permanency to the colony of Liberia, except from the light reflected by constant and continued emigration; and it is believed, by many shrewd philanthropists whose efforts have been long devoted to the cause of African colonization, that should emigration to the colony cease, the Negroes there would immediately relapse into their former habits and customs, and ultimately resume their original character of cannibals.

THE AFRICAN NOT INTENDED FOR FREEDOM.

No race will remain slaves which the God of nature intended, or which is fit, to be free; and it is the history of the African in this country, that the more fit to be free the more he is inclined to remain a slave. That portion of the African race here which have been most benefited by our civilization, scorn the false philanthropy which would restore them to barbarism, and beg the immunity of perpetual thralldom. This is a clear proof that the African is not intended for freedom, and at the same time shows that *instinct* teaches him, as it teaches all our domestic animals, to know the path of safety better than it can be learned in the school of fanaticism, or from the dialect of fools.

It is, therefore, in the philosophical aspect of the subject, in which it should be viewed, since philosophy searches down into the deep recesses of nature, and drags to light those hideous deformities of a race of barbarians, whose inherent passions revel in a sphere infinitely beneath the dignity of our domestic animals, and from whose frenzied rage for self-annihilation, enkindled by a morbid desire to devour their kind, the gentler beasts of the forest turn away in disgust, and humanity shrinks back with unmitigated horror!

BARBARISM SHOULD SUBSERVE CIVILIZATION.

To say, then, that it is JUST that barbarism should subserve civilization is a laconical axiom, which decides a plain question of right and wrong. The wrong is, that the African is a barbarian, and devours his kind; the right is, that in his service due and rendered to civilization, he receives its protection, and is compelled to forego the, to him, exquisite pleasure of devouring his kind. It will be observed that this view of the subject justifies, not only the perpetuation, but the inception of slavery, and renders emancipation absurd and cruel, and the inception of slavery just; leaving the continued transfer of barbarians to the midst of civilized communities, a right, the exercise of which could not involve or sacrifice any right of the barbarian, but must depend upon the enlightened decision of civilization, as to the reciprocal benefits to be derived therefrom. The conscience of civilization is the tribunal at which to try barbarism, as well as every other grade of inferior subjective existence. It stands above and controls all below it. The conscience of civilization decides both the right to summon the barbarian, and to hold him subject to its dictates; to weigh the benefits to civilization against the evils resulting from the adoption of the element of this super-animal force as an aid to civilization. Civilization deciding to take and hold the barbarian, it becomes right by the decision of the highest arbiter. The taking of the barbarian, and his employment as an adjunct of civilization, being in consequence of his moral delinquency, and his consequent mental imbecility, is no arrogation of right, because it is just; it is no assumption of right, because the empire of right is universal; it is no violation of right, because the act in itself is the exercise of the prerogative of right, of justice, in civilization, to suppress wrong and compel it to subserve right. In this view emancipation is no less unjust to the African than opposed to the law of right. To sieze him and drag him away to barbarism, against his will, is an act in favor of barbarism and in violation of right.

It restores to barbarism its victim, and robs the African of his supposed natural prerogative and choice, of service to civilization. The act, of itself, is the abnegation of that same right which it is designed or intended to assert.

THE AFRICAN'S AVERSION TO COLONIZATION.

Go ask the African his opinion of Liberia! Consult him as to the choice of his future home. He looks upon this land as a paradise, and upon that with instinctive dread and apprehension. Go ask the very slaves of the inventor of Central American Colonization (that devout apostle of *political philanthropy*, and most zealous advocate of emancipation), go ask *his slaves* their opinion of the merits of their master's invention, and their faces will kindle with the half ingenuous blush of conscious degradation, as they denounce his project, as the last device of insolence to degrade and oppress them.

IMPRACTICABILITY OF COLONIZATION.

The impracticability of African colonization* had long since become a foregone conclusion, so far as it could be made applicable to the present or prospective transfer of 4,000,000 of negroes from this republic to Liberia. A mathematical solution of that problem shows the cost of purchase and transportation to be no less a sum than $2,400,000,000, or ten times the amount of all the gold and silver coin in the United States. The purchase of

* Witness the following extract from the Report of the Committee of the Maryland Legislature in 1860, recommending the discontinuance of the annual appropriation of $5,000 to the Colonization Society for the purpose of sending free Negroes back to Africa. It will be seen by this extract, that the expense of transporting Negroes to Africa is much greater than I have stated, owing, perhaps, to an extravagant use or waste of the money by the Colonization Society; for if it costs $500,000 to transport 300 Negroes, it would certainly cost $6,668,000,000 to send away the 4,000,000 of Negroes in the United States. Add to this the value of the Negroes, to be paid in remuneration to the owners for their property, $2,000,000,000, and the total cost of purchase and transportation, based upon the experience and the statistics of the State of Maryland, would be $8,668,000,000! or more than forty times the amount of all the gold and silver coin in the United States! It will be seen that my own is a

these Negroes, alone, would cost $2,000,000,000, or eight times the amount of all our coin; and if we add to this the cost of transportation to Central America, the entire cost would not be less than $2,200,000,000. It will be seen that one scheme is as practicable as the other; and the alternative remains, of either robbing the people of nearly half the States of the Union of their property, or the Negro must remain a slave. No sane man will say that the purchase of this property is practicable or possible. Fancy, if you please, the Negroes bought and paid for; the estates of all the people of this country involved in the vain chimera of transferring to our Southern States, in remuneration, all the coin in Europe and America, and all that will be added thereto in a hundred years to come, and you have a picture not very suggestive of practicability or expediency.

But, even if the citizens of our Southern States should magnanimously propose the totally improbable act of voluntary and gratuitous manumission of their slaves, for the purpose of elevating them to political equality, what would be the effect upon our country? Three millions and a half of Negroes let loose upon our community, in competition, in the main departments of industry, with free white labor. Or would you, in accordance with the legislation of many of the States, exclude the negro from the

---

low estimate compared with this, and either of those estimates shows the utter futility of the advocacy of emancipation. That Report says:—

"The passage of the act of 1831, ch. 281, was framed with the design of removing our free Negroes beyond the limits of this State. But experience has shown that they will not willingly leave us. That act has been in operation for twenty-seven years, at an expense to the State of about $280,000, raised by taxation upon our citizen population. It is safe to say that $75,000 more has been cleared by the profits in trade to the coast of Africa in that time; and that $145,000 has probably been bestowed by voluntary contribution for the same object—making in all the sum of $500,000. And yet, with all this vast outlay of money, not over *three hundred free Negroes* have been removed. Slaves to a larger number have been set free and sent to Africa. During the last year not one single free Negro was sent to Africa from this State. When this law went into effect, we had 52,000 free Negroes in the State; and, after a trial of twenty-seven years, we now have 90,000 or 100,000. The inefficiency of this enterprise being so obvious to every one of the least reflection, your committee propose the repeal of all laws taxing the people for colonization purposes."

Northern, Middle, and Western States, and the Territories, and thus, by confining him to the South, give him political preponderance over the white man in many of the States of the Union? Imagine the pure crystal pillars of this temple of freedom turned to ebony; the radiant eyes of Freedom's Goddess shocked at the gloomy spectacle of symbolic night, and suffused with tears at such a desecration of her shrine!

GRADUAL OR PROSPECTIVE EMANCIPATION.

There is another popular idea of emancipation, which is unjust, fallacious, and impossible of application. It is known by the specious though plausible appellation of gradual or prospective emancipation; by which it is proposed to destroy, by legislation, the productiveness and the value of this species of property, after a limited period, by declaring the *confiscation of its increase*. This has been tried by mistaken philanthropy, or by organized duplicity, with no other effect but to transfer the slaves from State to State, and from the North to the South; but while this process has been going on, the number of slaves in the United States has increased more than four-fold,—from less than one to more than four millions. This is emancipation with a vengeance. In this ratio, prospective or gradual *emancipation* would give us, in seventy years more, 16,000,000 slaves. It will be seen that this process is not emancipation, but merely transposition, or change of locality. The very name of emancipation, thus applied, is a misnomer.

OF PARTIAL LEGISLATION.

But of the injustice of that partial legislation which would discriminate against the property of one class of citizens, to destroy its value, by proposing the confiscation of its increase, or excluding it from the State,—this is oppression. It may be submitted to, but it is unjust, partial legislation, and an arbitrary act of tyranny, and if persisted in will, some day, lead to war. Be-

2

18

sides, it does not effect the purpose intended. It does not diminish slavery, but only changes its locality. What would be said if it were attempted to invalidate any other species of property, by the confiscation of its increase, or an attempt to legislate it out of the State? To declare by legislation a forfeiture of rents of houses or lands, after a specified period, or the increase of any species of stocks, or other property? What is this but agrarianism? what but the first blow of the *levelers?* And if this is done with impunity, how long before some other species of property, in the shape of fancied *superfluous* individual wealth, will also be confiscated? There is no safety in establishing such a precedent.

PURPOSES OF BRITISH EMANCIPATION.

Emancipation contemplates the social and political equality of the races. It proposes to mix the pure Anglo-Saxon blood with the dark blood of Ethiopia! It proposes the amalgamation of civilization with barbarism. It proposes the debasement and downfall of this Republic, and the erection upon its ruins of a mighty military despotism. The alienation of that friendly sentiment and brotherly affection which existed among our people in the days of the Revolution, is prophetic of this; and unless reason resume her seat, and the convulsed sea of American mind, now lashed to fury by blind zealots and European emissaries among us, be calmed, and the angry wave of fanaticism be stayed, such will most certainly be the sad and startling consummation.

OF THE RIGHT TO ENSLAVE THE BARBARIAN.

It is pretended by certain sophists and visionary theorists, that the RIGHT does not exist to enslave the barbarian; that to assert such right is fatal to the principle of human equality. To which I answer, that barbarity is not humanity, but its opposite, and the right of the one to control the other is supported by law, founded upon the immutable principles of justice. The experience of mankind has demonstrated, and the judgment of mankind has decided, that certain acts are wrong in themselves; that to kill is an act abhorrent to the soul of man, and as it is also a violation of natural right, the murderer shall die—that in his death an element of chaos and destruction, in him, is annihilated—and the principle or element of murder in the wicked be thereby repressed. Here is an instance wherein the right is asserted, to take, not only the liberty, but the life of an individual. Some deny this right, but they do not deny the right to deprive the murderer of his liberty. All will agree that the murderer shall, at least, be deprived of his liberty. So with other crimes. There is a tolerable agreement in civilized communities, that for certain crimes men shall be deprived of their natural right to freedom. So, the principle is established, that communities have the right to deprive men of their liberties. Laws are established and executed by this principle. Every State, and almost every small community, endorses this principle, and constantly illustrates it by the punishment of offenders against law, who are confined in jails and prisons. And it is folly to deny a right founded upon the universal usage and experience of mankind. So with nations. Did we not repress the wrong exercised against us by Mexico and Algeria? Did we not even deny the right of maritime isolation to Japan, on the score of cruelty or neglected hospitality to our shipwrecked mariners? Suppose she slay our ambassador, or our resident minister; would we not still further force upon her, in a summary manner, those well-known rules of law, and amenities of civilization, and principles of justice, which are proclaimed to be right by the united voice of nations?

We are considering the subject of the enslavement of the African race in this Republic. We are inquiring into the right of African Slavery. We have asserted the right of slavery, as founded upon the principle that universal right holds a just and hereditary control over wrong; and as the African is a race of barbarians, and barbarism is wrong, it follows that it is the right of civilization to hold the African subject to those rules of justice which pertain to civilization, and to protect him from the injustice, violence, and degradation, which are the concomitants of barbarism. To deny this is to deny the superiority of RIGHT over *wrong*. He who denies this, becomes the advocate of barbarism; for, barbarism being below civilization, he asserts its equality with civilization, and thus becomes its apologist and advocate.

VIOLATION OF NATURAL RIGHT.

Such an one will claim that involuntary labor performed by the African, in behalf of civilization; or the production, by his labor, of material or fabrics to hide his nakedness, or adorn the human race, or protect them from the cold, degrades the barbarian, because it encroaches upon his natural right to go naked and houseless, and perish with the cold. He is quite *primitive* in his ideas of dress, and ought to emigrate to a warm climate, like South Africa or South America, where the elements of nature do not conspire with civilization to degrade and oppress him. He perceives that our unjust and oppressive laws actually punish, as an offense, the exposure to view of man's natural external beauties! This is about as far as it is safe to go on the subject of natural right, both from considerations of propriety and modesty, and also, as it almost amounts to a digression from the subject immediately under consideration; but we are merely following the advocate of emancipation, on the score of equality and natural right, just where his principles lead him; and as it forcibly suggests the inexpediency of emancipation, and consequent barbarism, on the score of morality and decency, it seems entirely apposite to the subject.

But it is claimed by some, that the African slave here has ceased to be a barbarian, which I deny. His nature is not essentially changed; his habits are forced; and he would at once fall, as he has fallen, and is falling, in San Domingo, Jamaica, and

Canada, but for coercion. It is, therefore, an external power which holds him up, and no innate principle within him.

THE DEBT OF THE BARBARIAN.

But even for argument, admitting the African were civilized, still he is not legally entitled to his freedom. Why? Because on account of his barbarism he became the property of another, who has a vested right in him. His transition from barbarism to civilization was at the expense of civilization, and he owes a just equivalent therefor. His debt is the difference between barbarism and civilization, and will be estimated according as the one is held higher than the other.

THE RIGHT OF THE AFRICAN TO REMAIN A SLAVE.

If the African is entitled to his freedom, he is also entitled to the privilege of remaining in servitude; a privilege which nine tenths of the Negroes in this country are well known to crave. But we deny his right of choice in the premises. His barbarism was the oblivion of his right to choose his own proper position; and the absence of inherent right in him subjects him at once to the dominion of universal or external right in civilization. His right of choice, therefore, has no real validity, and should not even be tolerated to denounce the heinous wrong of his emancipation, and consequent restoration to barbarism. His right to remain a slave is not his own, but the right of civilization; and even his willingness to remain in servitude, though a double evidence of his barbarism and of his appreciation of his partially ameliorated condition as an accessory of civilization, is not available in deciding as to his present or future condition; because the right exercised in his subjection to the rules of civilization is primordial, and sovereign, and all-controlling, as Universal Right, and is in no case subject to the will of barbarism.

THE MELIORATION OF THE AFRICAN.

With regard to the degradation of the African slave, that is admitted; but at the same time his position as an accessory to civilization is far higher than that wherein he was wholly the subject of barbarism. Now, he is dignified to the useful avocations of the civilized race; learns their rudimental arts and customs, and methods of subsistence; is subject to, and protected by law; becomes semi-civilized, and in rare, individual instances, as a *lusus naturæ*, even aspires to the nobler prerogatives of mind. The meanest slave that wears the shackle or feels the whip of civilization, in the reluctant performance of coerced labor, is a far nobler being than the African barbarian in his native wilds.

OF THE DEGRADATION OF LABOR.

Labor degrades no man. Labor is honorable, because the products of labor feed and clothe the world, and thus conduce to the welfare and happiness of mankind. Coerced labor is better than no labor. Coercion itself does not necessarily degrade man; rather may it ennoble and elevate, when it is exercised to summon the barbarian to the lessons of civilization. Coercion degrades not the man whom it compels to do right; it only exposes that degradation which is the result of doing wrong. The man only is degraded who, voluntarily or by coercion, does wrong, or neglects to do right. To talk of the degradation of labor, whether coerced or free, is, therefore, preposterous.

HUMAN EQUALITY.

But the question of emancipation is started and agitated on the ground of human *equality*. It is the supposed equality of the African with the white race, that is the pretext for emancipation, and the foundation of the assumed right and expediency of emancipation. It has been supposed by some, that the enunciation of human equality in the American Declaration of Independence was intended for all the races of men in the world. Such a supposition is totally unfounded, and unwarrantable in the very nature of things. In the first place, it is not true; and in the next place, the writer of that Declaration meant no such thing, for he held slaves, and knew their inferiority. What a monstrous act of hypocrisy and folly it would have been in the author of that instrument, and his cotemporaries, to declare that all men are created *free* when they knew millions are born slaves, or when they knew no *equality* existed, even of right, between the barbarian and the man whose sense of justice and perception of RIGHT secured to him the approbation of Heaven and his own conscience, by a recognition of and obedience to the laws of morality, and conformity to the just rules of civilization. They wrote that Declaration for white men,—meaning white men,—because it did not and could not apply to the barbarous and savage nations. They saw the world in chains, and knew the bondage of mankind to be the result of their violation of moral right, and their incapacity for self-government. They estimated rightly when they announced freedom to the white race in these colonies; for, up to this time, the fact of self-government by our people has verified their prophetic annunciation; but the sages who founded this Republic, excluded, by legislation, the African and the Indian from this boon of freedom, and they and their descendants have held the African in the condition of servitude.

INCAPACITY OF THE MINGLED RACES FOR SELF-GOVERNMENT.

The question of the enfranchisement of the African, therefore, involves the question of the capacity of the mingled races for self-government; a problem which is already solved in Mexico, in Jamaica, in San Domingo, and several of the Spanish American States. There, the mixed races have no common bond of union. The predominance of one petty State, or military chieftain, is the signal for the semi-barbarous hordes of mingled races to combine for the purpose of destruction. Urged on by the emissaries of that colossal superstition which casts its shadow over this Republic (whose home is a foreign kingdom, and whose head is a foreign prince), the semi-barbarous hordes of mingled races in the South American States, are a prey to successive bloody revolutions, through that imbecility which is the sure result of the amalgamation of civilization with barbarism.

WRONG SHOULD SUBSERVE RIGHT.

In considering the subject of slavery, there is one principle which must not, and cannot be lost sight of, as it underlies all else, and is the root from which springs the tree of all knowledge on this subject, as well as all others; to wit: That RIGHT holds a just and hereditary control over *wrong*. Not because right is the strongest, but because it is the BEST. It is very common when right asserts its prerogative, that we hear the subjects and votaries of *wrong* denounce RIGHT as mere *might*. This is a common foible of vice, to conceal its own deformity; a mere subterfuge, which, when pushed to the wall, vice adopts, and meets the executioner of justice with the accusation that he is the mere instrument of might; the servile tool of arbitrary power. This glozing of vice avails not. Justice stands erect in the dignity of its own moral beauty, and commends itself to the intellect and conscience of mankind. All the affections, all the wisdom, and all the experience of men, do homage at the shrine of justice, as the arbiter of right. This great moral tribunal, established at the dawn of creation, has existed through all time, and still exists; and at this tribunal we try barbarism, and find it to be wrong, because it conduces to the misery and degradation of men. At this tribunal, we find civilization to be right, because it conduces to the happiness and welfare of mankind. This being so (and the man who denies it, is a barbarian), it follows, that civilization, carrying with it the preponderating elements of right and justice, holds a just and hereditary control over barbarism, which is wrong. When we assert, therefore, the right of slavery, because it is just that barbarism shall subserve civilization, we only say it is just that wrong should subserve right;—a proposition, which, certainly, ought to commend itself to the common sense, the intellect, and the conscience of every good man.

Some assert that civilization should subserve barbarism; but when tried by our rule, they at once see that it is preposterous to assume that right should subserve wrong.

FORFEITURE OF NATURAL RIGHT.

Some propose, that the advantages of the great and little, the served and the servant, the good and the bad, should be reciprocal ; that that which is used is, or should be, as much advantaged in the using as is the user. I would ask them—what particular advantage it is to the oyster to be devoured? or what return can the earth make to the sun for his rays, constantly poured upon it? Some assert that every human being is unqualifiedly endowed by nature with the right of individual freedom. This we deny. We assert that barbarism is not humanity, and cannot claim to exercise the prerogative of civilization, which it has ignored, or which it never knew. We assert that the murderer has forfeited that right ; and more than this, with the element of murder developed in him, originally, he never was entitled to freedom. Prisons, and even dungeons, are as necessary and proper as schools and colleges, but not more so than servitude to the barbarian. They are all appliances of right and justice and civilization, not to make the good subserve the bad, but to make the bad subserve the good.

TAKING THE EXCEPTION FOR THE RULE.

It will not do for men to pretend that they do not know which is right and which is wrong ; what is civilization and what is barbarism. The exception for the rule is as proper to adopt in the one case as in the other. We cannot condemn civilization for the incidents of bad government in some cases, false religion in others, and crime in others, when the general tenor of civilization is to protect the weak against the strong, give security to life and property, and by developing the intellect and cultivating the moral faculties, elevate and ennoble the race. Neither can we acquit barbarism if it affords occasional instances of *immoderate instinct*, closely approximating to intellect, or even intellect itself, and moral worth, or the absence of ferocity, or the presence of positive amiability, render it possible that the barbarian is not a fiend, or that he may be schooled to tolerable docility, while the general tenor of barbarism is to wrong, cruelty, violence, and self-annihilation.

PASSION; SYMPATHY MISAPPLIED.

Nor will it do to ignore reason, and adopt passion when we consider the subject of slavery. Passions have their uses, but how often they are perverted! Reason is sometimes perverted too, and never more than when exercised against truth, justice, and civilization, and in favor of barbarism. There is a false sympathy, amounting to passion, that is blindly lavished upon objects which neither need nor appreciate it. We often see it exercised in behalf of the brute animals, whose proper natures are totally unconscious of it; while their gentleness and quietude seem to rebuke this shallow, human sentimentality, as something wandering from its sphere, or as seed wasted upon the sand. Your sympathy has its legitimate uses, and it is against the economy of nature to misuse it, or bestow it upon natures foreign to its own. If we pity the slave because he is not like ourselves, we shall probably receive his pity, in return, for some weakness or power in us, that covers an abyss which he cannot fathom, and from which he turns away in terror. He is adapted to his place, and so are we, if we are content.

PERFECTION OF NATURE'S WORK.

It has been said, with how much truth let us consider,

" Where ignorance is bliss, 'tis folly to be wise ; "

the reverse of which is, " Where knowledge is bliss, 'tis folly to be ignorant." The first proposition was evidently intended for the Negro, and the last for the white man ; as intellectual pleasures and knowledge are esteemed highest by the latter, and animal pleasures by the former. Happiness is the aim of both; the difference is in the mode of attaining it, and the degree of it when attained. The negro is perfect in his kind. Sympathy will not make him a white man. Would you interrogate nature on the wisdom of her works? Would you denounce them as imperfect? Can you improve upon the architecture of the honey-bee, or the method of his distillation? or on nature's processes of germination and vegetation? Your cup of liquid poison is but a mean equivalent for his treasured nectar ; your hot-house culture yields nought for the beauties of Flora, nor the sweetness of her priceless perfumes. The spider would not be a butterfly even if you could give him wings. The power to fly would only enable him to spin his web in air, and obscure the sunlight. His own way is best, both for him and man.

THE NEGRO SATISFIED WITH HIS CONDITION.

Reason will bring all things right. We must take things as they ARE, not as fancy would paint them. It is of no use to get exasperated because the Negro is dark of skin, and because his inferiority and degradation adapt him to the rougher, or rudimental departments and pursuits of civilization. Pity for him on account of the labor which makes his sleep sweet, and his digestion perfect, is thrown away. He knows nothing of the ennui of sloth, nor the misanthropy of idle declaimers. He has his rude affections, and does not hate wrongs which he does not know nor feel, nor is he shocked at manacles which he cannot see, and which hold him from falling into the abyss of barbarism, whence they have lifted him. He loves his condition as a slave to civilization, because his instinct tells him it is better than subjection to the usages and wrongs of the condition from whence he has risen. If he is satisfied with his present condition, it is from an intuitive instinct, teaching him his fitness for it, and shows, by the slowness of the transition from barbarism to civilization, how wide and deep is the gulf which divides the one from the other.

UNITY OF THE AFRICAN RACES.

I use the term barbarism in contradistinction to civilization, and very respectfully refer to authorities of repute in justification of this use of the word, both to designate the quality of the *thing*, and the precise locality of its fittest application; for although Herodotus tells us that the Egyptians and Greeks applied the term *barbari* to all who spoke a language different from their own; and even the Hindoos used almost the same word to express the quality indicated, differing only by the accidental dissimilarity of the Sanskrit orthography, which makes it *varvvarah* or *varvvaras*, we have the authority of Professor Wilson, who says it means "an outcast, and in another sense, woolly or curly haired, as the hair of the African." And for authorities showing the unity of the Negro races, dialects, and languages, in Western, Southern, and Central Africa, I refer to the writings of Progart, Ritter, Oldendorf, Marsden, Brusciotti, Harves, Grandpre, Vater, Salt; Ludolf, and Oldfield; who, from other motives than those which have prompted the partial accounts of more recent travelers and writers on the subject, have shown conclusively, that the degrees of barbarism existing in the tribes inhabiting the Western and Southern coasts of Africa, and the interior, are, in fact, mere modifications of that same barbarism, produced by local causes, and mitigated only by the force of nature from without, rather than by any inherent quality belonging to any portion of the Negro race. I speak of language as the connecting chain which links together the various African tribes, showing, if not their identity, their immediate connection, and holding to the account of barbarism those exceptions to the rule of barbarism which suggest the pretext for breaking down the barriers which divide barbarism from civilization, and form the basis of all the false philanthropy and efforts of political emancipation which are the curse of the age and country in which we live.

According to Pritchard, and others familiar with the subject, the slaves exported from Congo, which was long the principal resort of the Portuguese traders in black men, have always been regarded by slave-dealers and planters as genuine Negroes. If the physical traits of the Mapoota tribe, who will, as I suppose, be admitted to be undoubtedly of the Kafir race, so fairly represent the Negro character, it will be less difficult to admit that the natives of Mozambique and Congo belong to the same stock. All the inhabitants of the great empire of Congo speak one language, though it is divided into a number of dialects, including the dialect of Loango in the *north*, that of Congo in the south, and *Banda*, or idiom of Cassanga, in the interior, forming, collectively, one nearly allied family of languages, or, in fact, one language.

TRAVELERS IN AFRICA.

Since emancipation contemplates the transfer of the slaves to Africa, as the means of mitigating those supposed evils to which they are subjected, having already established by way of derision a *republic* there, I deem it legitimate to make some inquiry into the nature and condition of the inhabitants of Africa, in order to ascertain if such a change would be expedient or proper, with a view to the amelioration of the condition of the slaves. Of course, to do this, we must take the general authorities of history, and not confine ourselves to those individual authorities of recent date, which may be influenced by the popular delusion of *Negro equality*, or, for purposes of *gain* or from *political motives*, have *written books to sell*, or been *employed for pay* to belie the KNOWN TRUTHS OF HISTORY.

CANNIBALISM.

With regard to cannibalism, I demand that the advocates of emancipation either adopt it as right and proper, or denounce it, as I do, as beneath the dignity of ordinary animal existence, and as the most disgusting prerogative of barbarism. Probably they will adopt it on the very antique authority of Zeno, Diogenes, Chrysippius, and the Stoics, who esteemed it perfectly reasonable for men to devour one another; or because, in China (and other countries) it is practiced, where, according to Herrara, one great market is supplied with human flesh alone, for the better sort of people; or because cannibalism was universal before the days of Orpheus. I almost fear lest the emancipationists, by adopting cannibalism as right, with such high authorities and precedents to support their position, may endeavor to palliate African cannibalism on the ground that it is not a monopoly, and claim exemption from the great verdict of modern civilization which denounces, as forfeited and condemned, this disgusting and leading custom of barbarism. But if the common sense of the Anglo-Saxon race did not almost universally denounce this hideous custom, I would bring Sextus Empiricus to show that the first laws ever enacted were to prevent men from devouring each other; and even this may be declared, by our sophistical emancipationists, to be one of the first violations of *natural right*. If the right of cannibalism is claimed, then will nature assert its wrong, and vindicate civilization. But if cannibalism is rejected by the emancipationists, then let us see to what dangers and degradation he would expose the now happy and contented slave.

CANNIBALISM IN AFRICA.

In the "UNIVERSAL VOCABULARY," which is compiled from the very highest authority (p. 218), we learn that the Jagas, of the kingdom of Congo, "take pleasure in *eating young women!*" And "a princess was so fond of her gallants, that *she ate them successively!*" "Their choicest food is *warm human blood!*" "The Jaga chieftain, Cassangi, used to have *a young woman killed every day for his table!*" "Five or six strong men will at once destroy and share the flesh of a captive." "The women are equally as ferocious as the men, *delighting to cleave the skull, and suck the warm brains of the slain!*" This is solemn history, though almost horribly incredible.

From the same authority, and others, we learn that seven-eighths of Africa is at present either savage or barbarous. This is *the present condition of Africa*, by nearly the unanimous voice of enlightened travelers, and scientific explorers.

According to Pritchard, " the Mumbas, a numerous and savage people who live at the east and northeast of Te-te, and at Chicorango, are cannibals."

Dos Sanctas says, "They have in their principal town a slaughter-house, where they butcher men every day."

We learn from Pritchard, that " the Zimbas, or Mazimbas, are a man-eating tribe near Sena." Also, that "the Múlúa tribe slaughter fifteen or twenty men every day."

It is a well-authenticated fact, that the subjects of the Great Macoco are anthropophagi, or cannibals. "This prince has a court so numerous, as to require two hundred men to be butchered every day to supply his table ; a part of them criminals, and a part slaves furnished in the way of tribute." It is a part of history, both ancient and modern, that in the market-places in the principal towns and large villages throughout southern, and in portions of central Africa, Negro flesh is sold by the pound, as commonly as beef or mutton is sold throughout these United States; and what is worse, it is only the wealthy or more *intelligent* classes who are able to indulge in so great a luxury ; while the poorer classes, the mass of the people, are envious spectators of the traffic in this so great a luxury, as to tempt them to every violence and crime to enable them to indulge in it.

SUPREMACY OF PAGANISM IN AFRICA.

This is the fate to which emancipation would consign the Negro. These are a few of the selected examples of the horrors of barbarism, furnished by historians, scientific travelers, and

Christian missionaries, whose testimony, as eye-witnesses, has become history during the last few hundred years. Meanwhile, the light of civilization has blazed upon Africa from three quarters of the globe, even as the rays of the sun have enveloped the globe itself. Missionaries from Europe and America, from Rome, and London, and New York, have striven with a zeal and fidelity known only to religious enthusiasm, incited by mutual emulation, and armed with those terrors which awe the soul, those allurements which beguile the affections, and those fascinations which enkindle hope; but they have striven in vain against the colossal power of barbarism; and to-day, those heathen orgies which have darkened the annals of the world for four thousand years, are as sacred, to paganism in Africa, as are the rites and ceremonies of Christianity in London or in Rome.

Is this no evidence of the unfitness of the African for civilization? And is it just, in the sight of heaven, to force him from his present willing position of service to civilization, and consign him to a fate more terrible than even death itself!

THE AFRICAN RACE ON THIS CONTINENT.

Look at the African race on this continent, in this Republic, in Canada, and in the Islands of San Domingo and Jamaica. Compare the African in this Republic, under the wholesome regimen of civilization, with his emancipated brethren in the West Indies, or his recusant, fugitive brother in the Canadas. Has he not advanced here, and retrograded there? Compare his condition in these States, North and South. Why do the free States enact laws to prohibit the African from coming into them to settle? Is it because he is a civilized man, an equal, and a good citizen? Is it not rather, because the Anglo-Saxon race shuns the supposed contamination of barbarism? The wisdom of these prohibitory laws will be seen in the future time; when the idea of Negro equality has become exploded and obsolete; after the question of emancipation has served its purpose in political combination ; but alas ! not until the fallacy of negro equality has resulted in a mongrel race which will have spread itself like the shadow of a cloud over some of the fairest portions of freedom's heritage.

THE AFRICAN IS DEEMED A BARBARIAN IN THE NORTHERN STATES.

It will be seen that the arguments here advanced are predicated, to some extent, upon the fact that the African is a barbarian. That he is so in his native wilds, we have shown by high authority. That he is so in this country, is obvious, from the fact that in the South he is held a slave, and is satisfied with his condition ; and because, as a race, the African in this country, and on this continent, shows not the least capacity for self-control. In the South, the African, in his best estate, is a slave. In the North, laws are wisely enacted to prevent him from going there, because of his barbarism, and because that portion of the most advanced race on earth shrinks from contact with it. The fact, then, of his barbarism is sustained, fully,—by his normal condition in Africa ; his condition of retrogradation in Jamaica and San Domingo, where the experiment of emancipation has proved a failure, where the relapse into barbarism is sure and irrevocable ; and in this country, where common sense and public opinion and public law, both North and South, hold him in the condition of social, moral, and physical vassalage and servitude, and confine him effectually within certain prescribed limits, or hold him in that marked estimation of inferiority which makes him forever conscious of his own degradation. I have felt justified, therefore, not by way of opprobrium, nor in the spirit of invidious or odious comparison, to name the category in which he belongs, and then, by fair moral and philosophical argument to deduce the justice and right of civilization in holding dominion over him.

EMANCIPATION IS WRONG.

It is not our purpose to blame the African for being a barbarian ; but to insist that emancipation is wrong because it restores

him to barbarism, and that slavery is right because it holds him
to those rules of justice which pertain to civilization, and protects
him from the injustice, violence, and degradation which are the
concomitants of barbarism. As the slave of civilization, he is
raised infinitely above his former condition as the subject of barbarism. He knows this, and is satisfied. His instinct teaches
him to love his master, because he is his protector, and because,
mistrusting his own capacity for self-government, he knows the
necessity for a master; and instances are numerous, of slaves,
having misjudged their own capacity for self-government, having
fled from supposed wrongs, they found they were mistaken as to
the means of bettering their condition, and returned to voluntary
servitude, begging, with tears, to be again admitted to the sacred
precincts of the patriarchial care.

FITNESS OF THE AFRICAN FOR SLAVERY.

It is the fitness of things that makes the African a slave. His
brawny limbs, seconding and aiding the intellect of the superior
race, constitute the left hand and foot of labor. Slavery is the
left hand of our body politic. Free labor is the right hand.
Intellect is the head. All combined, constitute a power which is
felt and feared by the foes of this Republic. Hence their endeavor to detach one portion from the other, and thus weaken the
whole. To change the position of the slave is to interrupt or
reverse the order of nature.

> "What if the foot, ordained the dust to tread,
> Or hand to toil, aspired to be the head?
> What if the head, the eye, or ear repined
> To serve, mere engines of the ruling mind?
> Just as absurd for any part to claim
> To be another in this general frame;
> Just as absurd to mourn the tasks or pains
> The great directing Mind of All ordains."

ABSURDITY OF NEGRO EQUALITY.

The truth is, slavery is right, and is proved to be so, notwithstanding all the noisy declamation we hear about human equality. The Negro is a barbarian, and barbarism is not humanity but inhumanity; hence the unfitness to the case, of such illogical reasoning as is adopted by the advocates of Negro equality. Human equality, as applied to the Negro, is an idle fantasy, without even the shadow or semblance of plausibility. White men are equals in few things; certainly not in physical nor mental capacity, nor power. The equality declared by our Revolutionary Sires was the political equality of white men. Let us arise from that lethargy in which we have dreamed of universal equality, and escape the dangers of that moral and intellectual somnambulism in which we have been groping to the verge of social and political destruction.

AMERICAN AND EUROPEAN RADICALISM.

This restless spirit of change, in a portion of our people, this craving for universal equality, by the blind victims of popular fanaticism, finds its parallel in the destructive element of European radicalism, (that bane of European democracy,) which mistakes freedom for the right of plunder, and Democracy for the right of popular despotism. It is that blind spirit of rage which adapts not the means to the end, but overreaches itself, and falls a prey to its own cupidity, duplicity, and folly.

INEQUALITY OF RACES.

Universal equality,—the equality of the African with the Caucasian, or the savage with the civilized races, is no more possible than to blend right with wrong. The inequality exists in nature, as indubitably as the varied magnitudes of the stars. And the characteristics of the various savage races differ as widely as their varied physiognomy. There is no equality among them, mental or physical,—not even equality of degradation. The gigantic Patagonian, and the dwarfish Laplander; the wild Feejeeian, and docile Guinea Negro; the stolid Indian, and ant-like plodder of teeming India,—are but the outward symbols of that contrariety of moral, or rather immoral existence which is the fate of barbarism. They have no equality of beauty nor ugliness, leanness nor obesity, vice nor virtue, but varying differences, such as the spontaneous growth of uncultured nature in different climes exhibits in the vegetable and lower orders of the animal creation. What a contrast is this to that trained, drilled conformation to the order and proper conventionalities of civilized life, which our free schools, free press, social rites, laws, and customs impose.

QUIBBLE OF THE SOPHIST.—TAKING THE EXCEPTION FOR THE RULE.

And here comes the quibble of the sophist, who singles out instances of law violated in civilized communities, and holds them up as the criterion by which to judge civilization, and triumphantly exclaims, Lo! the fruits of civilization—of that civilization which arrogates to itself the right to enslave mankind! But this is merely a base perversion of truth. He deceives no one so much as himself, when he imagines the world will take the *exception* for the RULE of civilization, or make it the pretext to sustain barbarism.

THE SUPREMACY OF MIND OVER MATTER.

It is safe to assert that right holds a just and hereditary control over wrong. *Veritas vincit.* Justice and truth go hand in hand. Barbarism must bow before the genius of civilization. And what is not found in international law, nor suppressed by it, nor dictated by the commercial rivalries of nations, nor the jealous diplomacy of kings, will yet continue as it ever has, to recognize the power of mind over matter, of reason over passion, of intellect over animal existence; and the dominion and supremacy of written constitutions over citizens, communities, States, and empires. The right of government in civilized States more than suggests the right and supremacy of civilization over barbarism.

But the right of mind over matter, of intellect over mere animal life, of reason over passion, is asserted upon the broadest principles of philosophy in nature. The Infinite Spirit, unseen, moves the visible material creation as the creature of his will.

> He framed the universe, and instant twirled
> Upon its orbit, this terrestrial world ;
> Bid chaos flee, and called the glittering train
> Of constellations to the ethereal plain ;
> He built the fabric of creation fair ;
> Lit every sun that shines in glory there ;
> Strewed with his hand, to deck heaven's argent fields,
> Each starry atom that refraction yields ;
> And holds in order, as it moves along,
> Each seraph bright, of the celestial throng!

SHALL BARBARISM CONTROL CIVILIZATION?

Behold the order of heaven! Does any passion bear sway there? The ponderous globes obey the mandate of spiritual superiority; and shall the order of nature be reversed here, and the animal species lord it over man? Shall barbarism again come on the track of civilization, with fire and sword, and ruthless annihilation? Shall civilization invoke the demon of destruction to its own downfall? Shall the frenzy and rage of visionary enthusiasts, *or the dark schemes of the emissaries of despotism in this Republic,* lay in ruins this fair temple of freedom, the home, and refuge, and hope of the down-trodden nations?

THE RAGE OF PASSION.

What are these dreams of sophists, these vagaries of imagination, this rage of passion, this perversion of reason, and high-sounding declamation, confounding right with wrong, civilization with barbarism, but the paraphernalia of despotism arrayed against the liberties of mankind? Emancipation is all a delusion, a foible, a fantasy, an idle dream! The soul and intellect of man is heaven-derived, and knows its order and beauty, and will hold in abeyance these elements of chaos. The barbarian is indeed dark of skin, and the radiance of a million constellations in a thousand ages will not change him, nor the light of civilization fade to moral brightness his gloomy mind!

EMANCIPATION OF THE WHITE RACES.

It will be observed that my argument on the subject of slavery is new, and is drawn from the actual nature of the case. I offer no antique authority to sustain the RIGHT of slavery. The history of the African race for four thousand years is sufficient, which is, that in no country nor condition has that race shown the capacity for or enjoyed self-government. And, indeed, self-government with the superior white races is still deemed but an experiment. The great mass of the white races ever have been, and still are, governed by the strong hand of despotism, or by the more plausible, but ofttimes not less diabolical power of constitutional sovereignties, or hereditary or revolutionary oligarchies. It is not, then, so great a disparagement to the African that he is unfit for freedom, when nine-tenths of the foremost of the white races, show not the capacity to enjoy it. Certainly, the African is not their superior. Why, then, demand for him more than is allowed to the superior white races? If emancipation is to be thought of, would it not be well to emancipate the white races first?

THE ARGUMENT INVULNERABLE.

I have rested my argument on no antique authority to show the right of slavery. I have appealed to no religious dogmas to show this right. I have not even availed myself of the whole tenor of sacred history to justify it, which has been done heretofore by others, and done in vain. I have not labored to produce a voluminous collation of other men's opinions to swell my pages. Sacred history is in the hands of all, and its teachings need not my endorsement, recommendation, nor reiteration. Indeed, if the right of slavery here asserted is not based upon truth, and if it does not commend itself to the unbiased judgment of my countrymen, then I demand that they discard it. I ask if the argument here advanced, has been or can be refuted? If it can be, let it be done fairly, openly, and without circumvention. Let it be shown that barbarism ought not to subserve civilization. Let it be shown that civilization is wrong, because it does not conduce to the well-being and happiness of mankind ; let it be shown that barbarism is right because it does this. Let the apologists and advocates of barbarism show its equality with civilization. Let it be denied, and the denial proved, that the laws of universal right and justice hold true and heaven-derived supremacy over wrong. Let it be shown that the slave-owner has no legal right of property in his slaves. Or, if it be admitted that he has such right, let any possible process of emancipation be pointed out. Will the violent denunciations of fanaticism induce him to free his slaves? Does the divided sentiment and feeling evinced in even the division of the churches north and south, indicate the willingness of the owners to free their slaves? If not, then by what means are they to be set free? Is it to be by purchase? and if so, is it proposed to pay the value of the slaves? and how? Let it be shown that the purchase and transportation of 4,000,000 of Negroes to Africa will cost less than $2,400,000,000 ; or to Central America less than $2,200,000,000. Let it be shown to be expedient, practicable, or possible to do this; and even if done, let it be shown to be a benefit to the slave or the master ; a benefit either to civilization or barbarism.

If none of these things can be shown, and I aver they cannot, then how about the last startling alternative of robbing the slave-owner of his property? or the freeing of the Negroes by servile insurrection and civil war? What would be the cost in blood and treasure to effect this? and the probable result of *such* an effort at emancipation, on the freedom and civilization of the world?

WHY ENGLAND ABOLISHED THE SLAVE TRADE,—HER DREAD OF OUR GREATNESS AND POWER.

The truth is, the slave trade was abolished by British and Tory influence, at about the time of the American Revolution, when slavery, as an adjunct of colonial vassalage, could no longer subserve the interests of British commerce. This was their first success in circumventing us. Her complicity in the Cooley trade is an evidence of this. She is willing to morally damn herself for purposes of monarchical intrigue, in order to supplant us. Our agriculture and commerce, and rapidly accumulating wealth and power, and republican glory, are too much for her. Our example of success in freedom tempts the loyalty of the most enlightened subjects of the British crown. The fascinations of freedom beguile the ardent and noble aspirations of the English democracy, and Britannia, with her antiquated and wrinkled visage, shrinks abashed from the majestic presence of Freedom's immortal and fadeless bloom!

This is the true cause of the present British Negro philanthropy, and the occasion of her *assumed* moral turpitude in elevating the heathen barbarian of Africa to the primary plane of civilization, to the protection of its laws, and the meliorations of its moral, political, social, and religious institutions. It is because monarchy was beginning to be odious in the eyes of the European democracy, when contrasted with our antagonistical system of the divine right of the people. It is her policy and her purpose to render our institutions unstable by means of a suborned and venal press, and a band of mercenary, hireling, political and religious monarchical conspirators, parasites and traitors. These her gold can furnish. Her arms having repeatedly failed to subjugate the American democracy, she now has recourse to her diplomacy, her intrigues, and her gold. Twenty millions of money expended in this way in the last twenty years, has had its effect, and to her emissaries, and hireling presses and scribblers, we are indebted for a dastardly generation of traitors, who would barter the liberties of their country for the applause of faction, and the complacency of kings.

ENGLAND'S SELF-IMPOSED ODIUM.

It is a monstrous absurdity, nay it is an act of egregious hypocrisy, for England now to *assume* for herself an *hypothetical guilt*,—after bringing the African to her American Colonies for purposes of *gain*, and after exercising an intolerable tyranny over the white race in those colonies, and even invoking the aid of the tomahawk and scalping knife of the American savage in their attempted subjugation,—for the purpose now, when her arms and diplomacy have repeatedly failed, of seeking to overthrow the freedom of a Republic, which has risen, in despite of her, to such colossal proportions, as, in its very existence, to menace the combined monarchies of the world. But we hold these 4,000,000 of barbarians subject to the laws of civilization ; and let England remember that we, even now, have the magnanimity to relieve her from the self-imposed odium of doing right ! We now tell her monarchists, degenerate sons of illustrious sires, that in their maritime decadence they have also morally retrogaded, for they now seek to restore these Africans to barbarism !

SLAVERY IS AN INCIDENT OF CIVILIZATION.

Let it not be claimed, even as a sophistical subterfuge, that the *motive* which brought the African here was mercenary, and that, therefore, his coming here was not justifiable. Commerce is the handmaid of civilization, and if his coming was only incidentally right, yet that incident belongs to civilization, which is amenable to the moral code, and is also to be commended, with all its incidental, as well as more matured blessings. The institutions of civilization rescued these 4,000,000 of barbarians from the dangers, degradation, and miseries of barbarism, and by causing them to subserve civilization, compelled them to do right. The English and American false philanthropists, monarchical emissaries, ecclesiastical parasites, and psuedo-republican traitors now demand that these Africans shall be restored to barbarism, not because it is practicable or possible, or right, but because the proposition involves the equality of these States, and consequently the existence of the American Union. The success of these conspirators depends upon an adequate numerical proportion of knaves and monomaniacs, the well-adjusted mechanism of monarchy for the overthrow of this Republic. Their success would forever settle the long mooted question of the capacity of Anglo-Saxon race for self government. Hence the lavish employment of British gold to suborn the American press, and seduce the American mind from the safe precepts of Washington, whose name is, and ever has been, a terror to the British oligarchy.

SOLUTION OF THE SUBJECT.

The only tribunal at which to try human actions, is the tribunal of justice. That which is right can stand the test of this tribunal; that which is wrong will shrink in terror from it. At this tribunal American Negro slavery has nothing to fear, because it is founded in moral right. Its advocacy is the advocacy of right, and right alone; unless, forsooth, we are to confound right with wrong, and declare barbarism equal with civilization. Of course, our argument is based upon the hypothesis that civilization is one thing, and barbarism another. To the mind which is so mentally and morally obtuse as not to discover the difference between these two conditions, this appeal must be in vain. But to the right-minded man, who is open to conviction of truth, who has the mental freedom to act and think independent of his prepossessions and prejudices, who is guided by his intellect, and reason, and not by passion nor prejudice, this solution of the slavery question, though new, must and will be satisfactory, because it is the logical result of a trial of the question at the tribunal of justice and of rights, because slavery rescues the African from wrong, and subjects him to the rule of right;

because it rescues him from the wrongs and miseries of barbarism, and raises him to the *primary* elevation of a progressive and ennobling civilization.

EQUALITY OF THE STATES AND CITIZENS.

The equality of the sovereign States which compose the American Republic, and the equality of the citizens, both in the States and the Territories, constitute the true and only bond of union for the American people. This equality is the foundation stone upon which our whole social and political superstructure rests. To call this in question is to menace the very existence of the Union which is founded upon it. The sovereignty of the Union, extending over the Territories, where no other sovereignty exists, is the panoply of protection to all the inhabitants of the Territories. There they are all equal in person and property. There they are not sovereign, but subjects under the sovereignty of the united confederacy of States, which have no individual superiority and right in the Territories, neither for themselves, nor their citizens. For the inhabitants of such Territories to *assume* a sovereignty therein, not in accordance with the Constitution of the United States, not in conformity to law, and in violation of the equality of the people of the States there congregated, is USURPATION. Nor can the democracy of numbers, nor the will of the majority of inhabitants congregated in such Territories be invoked to decide the rights of the people of the several States congregated in such Territories, either as to persons or property; because the sovereignty of the Union holds, until superseded by the sovereignty of a State constitutionally organized, deriving its sovereignty from the supreme authority of the confederated States, by whose assent alone the primordial sovereignty of the Union is so far abandoned as to admit the exercise of State sovereignty in such Territories. There would be no propriety nor justice in allowing an *hypothetical sovereignty* to a few thousands of individuals congregated in a large Territory, not one

fiftieth part of which they occupied; allowing them to establish
a rule of exclusion of the persons or property of the people of a
portion of the States coming to settle in the Territories. Such
persons have neither the right to decide for the present, nor the
future; because at present they are not sovereign, and certainly
they should not be allowed to exercise a *usurped* authority over
the millions who shall occupy those Territories in the future. It
is a morbid desire to forestall the future, in its judgment of barbarism, and of its fitness to subserve civilization, that creates the
present animosity between the citizens of the different sections of
the Union, going into the Territories. This is all wrong. The
sovereignty of the Union is the present, and the sovereignty of
States the future arbiter of the rights of the people in the Territories; all other power is assumed, arbitrary, gratuitous, and in
violation of legitimate, delegated constitutional power.

The wisdom of the sages who founded the American Union
left nothing for experiment to their successors, so far as the absolute equality of American citizens is concerned; and there is no
safety but in the recognition of that perfect equality which the
spirit of our race demands, and which the power of the civilized
world will be invoked to maintain.

THE NECESSITY OF OUR ONWARD PROGRESS AS A NATION.

The intimate commercial relations existing between this Republic and the principal maritime and warlike nations of the globe,
mainly by means of the products of slave labor, constitute a
necessity for our onward, uninterrupted progress, as the great
agricultural and commercial almoner of civilization, and cannot
be disturbed, except at the peril of that civilization which they
have been so instrumental and conspicuous to promote. The proposed annihilation of the hand of labor whose products amount to
$250,000,000 per annum, and those products constituting the
articles of prime necessity to civilization, is a matter which
involves other interests than our own; and however willing mon-

archists and their minions may be to disrupt our political system, and destroy this temple of freedom, they will find the genius of commerce and the genius of liberty will continue to go hand in hand to uphold the principles of right and justice, which demand that barbarism shall subserve civilization.

AMERICAN COTTON.

American cotton, the product of slave labor, clothes, to a large extent, one-fourth part of the human race; without it the glory of civilization would vanish. It embellishes the denizen of the city, and hides the nakedness of barbarism. It is the tablet on which is inscribed the history of the present, and rescues from oblivion the mouldering records of the past. It is the talisman of thought, and the vehicle of those electric currents that blaze athwart the sky of mind, with which intellect binds together, with silver thread, the mind's great empire, where kings do homage at the shrine of genius, and bow in awe, and humble reverence before the majesty of mind. It is the medium through which the internal and external domains of thought are blended, and truth made universal, and obvious to the apprehension of a world!

WASHINGTON NOT OPPOSED TO SLAVERY AS WRONG.

It has been urged, that because Washington regretted the impossibility of devising some feasible means of emancipation, that, therefore, he was opposed to slavery, as wrong. The precise opposite was the case. He was too wise to oppose that which he could not overcome. His whole career was success in overcoming opposition. He might, with us, regret the barbarism of the African and the impracticability of his release from servitude, on account of his unfitness for freedom; but he never could logically or reasonably oppose, as wrong, that which made the African better and happier, and which protects him from the dangers and miseries of barbarism, though it placed him in the position to learn only the rudiments of civilization. To assert that Washington deemed slavery a wrong to the slave, is to accuse him of knowingly doing wrong, for he held slaves to the day of his death; and if he emancipated them then, it was more with the hope than the reasonable expectation, that even ms slaves, with all the force of his example during his whole life, had become fitted for freedom, or that they would be benefited by the experiment of their own attempted self-control. Washington could not, therefore, consistently oppose slavery as a wrong to the slave, nor conscientiously believe it to be wrong; because he would not oppose that which he could not overcome, and because his whole life was occupied in doing right. It is against the prophetic character of Washington's mission, ever crowned with success; against his wisdom, which was most profound; and against his judgment, which was unerring,—to presume his hostility to slavery as wrong, or his opposition to it in a moral point of view, when he knew, as we know, the emancipation of the slaves to be wrong in itself, and impossible, even if right or desirable. It is plain, then, that if Washington had any real aversion to Negro slavery, it was not because it was wrong so far as any natural right of the slave was involved, but because of his ability to do without slaves; and notwithstanding his fortune was ample, he *held* his slaves during the whole course of his life; whereas, if he had deemed slavery a wrong to the slaves, he would undoubtedly have granted them their liberty. What right would he have had, as a just man, to bestow his generosity upon the public, by refusing the emoluments of office, justly due him, and unjustly appropriating the proceeds or avails of the labor of his slaves, if he knew, or believed they were justly entitled to their freedom. If our moral view of slavery is clear, he was *just*, as well as *generous*, and wise as well as successful.

WASHINGTON REPROACHES THE EMANCIPATIONISTS.

It is well known how powerful the secret influence of the British and Tory abolitionists was in this country immediately after the American Revolution, as well as before and since that time; and that at about that time, or soon after, the question was seriously entertained of abolishing slavery in Virginia by legislation, as was done in other States of the Union; and it was on account of the annoying importunities of these *disinterested phil-anthropists* (?), and the apparent inclination of the people of the State of Virginia to experiment in their theories, that Washington expressed his willingness to see slavery abolished by legislative enactment. But in what characteristic terms of manly reproach did he address the Emancipation Society on the subject when he found their principles and practices to be that " *the end justifies the means.*" He says :

" *But when slaves, who are happy and contented with their present masters, are tampered with and seduced to leave them ; when masters are taken unawares by these practices ; when a conduct of this kind begets discontent on one side, and resentment on the other ; and when it happens to fall on a man whose purse will not measure with that of the Society, and he loses his property for want of means to defend it,—it is oppression in such a case,* AND NOT HUMANITY IN ANY, *because it introduces more evils than it can cure.*"*

OUR FATHERS ON THE RIGHT OF SLAVERY.

It is not to be concealed, however, that some of the sages who framed this Republic, in their zeal for freedom, overlooked the fact of African barbarism, or failed to be explicit in their unpremeditated enunciations of human freedom. Perhaps, however, they had more astuteness than has been supposed by some. Perchance they considered barbarity not humanity, but its opposite, and would have deemed it a work of supererogation to explain that which natural history, the history of the African race for four thousand years, and common sense, and common

* Scrœder's Max. of Washington, p. 256.

observation, had established as a self-evident proposition; to wit, that equality was a *political*, and not a social, nor moral, nor even physical condition; and that, especially, neither equality nor freedom were to be construed to be the prerogatives nor the right of barbarism. And the Constitution of the United States, the work of their own hands, sanctions this supposition, by recognizing the existence, and providing for the right of Negro slavery, and rescues the Fathers of the Republic from the absurd and opprobrious imputation of advocating Negro equality. Whatever opinions they may have expressed under the varying aspects of our Revolutionary epoch, the Constitution of these United States was the finality of their arduous toils, heroic achievements, and sublime wisdom; and that Constitution, the very sublimation and quintessence of a hundred civilizations, exhibiting the onward progress of the human race, recognizes the Right of Slavery, founded upon the immutable principles of justice.

MONARCHICAL SCHEMES TO DESTROY THIS REPUBLIC.

Is it strange, however, that since this Republic is the mighty antagonism of monarchy, and since it is invincible in arms, is it strange, that civil dissension, and the appropriate means to produce it, should be employed by despotism to subvert this government? What else should they do; What is the interest of monarchy in relation to the existence and onward progress of this Empire of Freedom? What, but its subversion, its disseverment, by its own internal antagonism? And what other means could monarchy and its parasites employ to accomplish this, but precisely the means and agency which have been employed, at vast expense, especially for the last twenty-five years, first to divide, and finally to destroy that which no external force, nor combination of external forces could subdue? Is it not already the boast of the minions of despotism that they have rendered our government insecure? With what jubilation did they catch the tidings of our recent rebellion, as the harbinger of their own redemption from the fate of political decadence and downfall, which our all-absorbing greatness was beginning to make so manifest to the willing apprehension of mankind? Their ears were charmed, even at the supposed triumphant voice of barbarism over a civilization as stable as the sun, which is immortal in its every individual microcosm, and to which they are conscious their own unequal systems of government never can attain.

OUR VINDICATION.

Need we inquire further what is the interest of monarchy? Can we any longer be blind to our own interest? Are we not arraigned at the tribunal of civilization, by the helots of despotism? Are we not accused of wrong? Are not we, and our sainted and godlike ancestors, held as amenable to moral law for a violation of Right? And shall we submit in silence to all this clamor; this false and slanderous accusation, when all history, all knowledge, all experience, all reason, and all nature, are voluble in our defense, and pronounce our just and triumphant vindication!

Let us, then, henceforth cultivate and encourage friendship and cordial co-operation between the different sections of the Union, and a patriotic emulation for its continuance; not upon any such visionary and deceptive hypothesis as the superiority and predominance of sectional partiality, but upon the equable and fundamental principles of justice, and of the absolute equality of these sovereign States, and the equality of the citizens of a well-compacted and glorious confederacy.

THE PHILOSOPHICAL POSTULATES OF AMERICAN SLAVERY.

1. Right holds a just and heaven-derived supremacy over wrong.

2. Barbarism is wrong. It conduces to the misery and degradation of mankind. Africa is barbarous. The African race is a race of barbarians.

3. Civilization is right. It conduces to the elevation and happiness of mankind.

4. Civilization carries with it the right of supremacy over barbarism.

5. It is right to summon the barbarian to the lessons of civilization, and to teach him its *primary* lessons; to elevate him to the dignity of labor.

6. It is right to HOLD the barbarian subject to the rules of civilization; to protect him by its laws, and rescue him from the wrongs and miseries of barbarism. In this way, only, he can be made happier and better. He falls, if unsupported by external power.

7. American Slavery promotes civilization by the production of materials wherewith to clothe the nakedness of mankind, and the useful medium of knowledge and intelligence, through books, and literature, printed upon materials which are the product of slave labor.

8. It is just that barbarism should subserve civilization; that Wrong should subserve Right.

9. The African is not equal to the white man, but is a barbarian, and as such has no political rights.

10. American Slavery is Right.

CONCLUSION.

If, then, it is not right, nor practicable, nor possible, to restore these 4,000,000 of Africans to barbarism, why any longer agitate the subject? Why keep the negro in perpetual dread of change, and the owner dubious of the future? Why, by this negro agitation, create apprehension in the minds of our own people for the stability and permanence of this government, and hope in the minds of all the monarchists of the world that this agitation will divide and destroy this last great bulwark of human freedom?

Why shall we put to hazard that freedom which is already secure? Why involve in experiments those tangible acquisitions which we have made to this priceless inheritance of freedom? Washington is gone, but he has left us his bright example, and his solemn admonitions. Let those who are greater, and wiser, and purer than Washington, impeach him. Let those whose precepts or examples excel his, question the superiority of his virtue and valor. Let those who have done more for human freedom, denounce him as the enemy of mankind, and erect for themselves a standard of moral action, which shall rise to the stupendous height of their own boundless egotism!

But if it is found to be inexpedient and wrong to agitate the subject of slavery, when it is known to be impracticable, impossible, and unjust to emancipate the slaves, then let us go on in our career of greatness, with success and tranquility. Let us watch with jealous care the honor of our country, and scorn the aspersions of its vilifiers. Let us honor and vindicate our country in its attitude of justice, and in its mission of civilization, and mark with the imputation of opprobium every recreant defamer of our government and its institutions. Let the emissaries of despotism find some other means of subduing us than to " divide and conquer." Let the name of Washington be revered; let his admonitions be heeded; let his commands be obeyed, and his example followed. Let barbarism still be blessed with the light of civilization; let the glory and dominion of freedom be established, and the citizens of this Republic rest in security and peace within their patriarchal bowers!